THE SWEET TASTE OF LIGHTNING

THE SWEET TASTE OF LIGHTNING

<po’ems and po’em·o·logues>

SHERI-D WILSON

ARSENAL PULP PRESS
VANCOUVER

THE SWEET TASTE OF LIGHTNING

ARSENAL PULP PRESS
103-1014 Homer Street
Vancouver, BC
Canada V6B 2W9
www.arsenalpulp.com

The publisher gratefully acknowledges the support of the Canada Council for the Arts for its publishing program, as well as the support of the Book Publishing Industry Development Program, and the B.C. Arts Council.

Printed and bound in Canada

CANADIAN CATALOGUING IN PUBLICATION DATA:
Wilson, Sheri-D.
The sweet taste of lightning

Poems.
ISBN 1-55152-060-5

I. Title.
PS8595.I586S88 1998 C811'54. C98-910874-0
PR9199.3.W4988S88 1998

CONTENTS

DIRECT HIT

YOU'RE MY LIQUOR I JUST WANNA GET PISSED ON YOU / 15

A ROOM WITH A WINDOW TO JUMP FROM / 17

SHE AND HER AND YOU AND ME ARE INSEPARABLE / 19

LEFT / 20

IF YOU GO INSIDE — YOU BETTER HAVE WRITTEN A WILL . . . / 21

WISHBONE AT TATE / 24

ZIG ZAG LIGHTNING

BUKOWSKI ON THE BLOCK AH-HA / 29

O HAIL THEE MIGHTY CABBY / 32

STAYING AT THE BALMORAL HOTEL / 34

THE NEW YORK WALDORF ELEVATOR GENIE BITCH / 36

FAST FOR-WORDS / 39

THIS POEM IS TO BE READ OUT LOUD / 41

SLEEPING IN THE AIR / 42

SHE DOESN'T KNOW SHE'S A DOG / 44

M.I.-5 SPY / 48

THE SWEET TASTE OF LIGHTNING / 52

LIFE BOLT

GINSBERG'S GONE GONE GONE / 55
AVUNCULAR / 58
INCH-BY-INCH / 59
HE WENT BY JOE / 62
FAMOUS LAST WORDS / 64

BALL LIGHTNING

NAILS AND LASHES / 69
THE DE SADE FAMILY ESCAPES SALTANA RESEARCH SITE . . . / 72
that crazy cat / 75
BUT THE SEX WAS GOOD / 77
ZEBRA FACES OF MEN WHO ESCAPED FROM THE ZOO / 78
HE WAS A HOTHEAD / 80

RED LIGHTNING

CONVERSATIONS WITH A CUNT / 87
THE ROOSTERS OF RAROTONGA / 92
I'M SICK OF BEING A SEX TRAINER / 94
FROM BUNHEAD TO BARD . . . / 97
. . . AND BACK AGAIN / 101

RAPID FLASH

MONTREAL MONTREAL AND ONLY MONTREAL / 109
OUI ET NON / 111

ACKNOWLEDGEMENTS

Some of these poems appeared in the following publications, recordings and performances: BUKOWSKI ON THE BLOCK AH-HA (*Poetry Nation: The North American Anthology of Fusion Poets*), YOU'RE MY LIQUOR I JUST WANNA GET PISSED ON YOU (*Scarabeus Vancouver-Paris*), OUI ET NON (performed with Decidedly Jazz Danceworks), O HAIL THEE MIGHTY CABBY (recorded by CBC for *Radio Sonic*), FROM BUN HEAD TO BARD (performed at the Kiss Project), . . . AND BACK AGAIN (performed with Springboard Dance Company), ZEBRA FACES OF MEN WHO ESCAPED FROM THE ZOO (recorded by CBC for *Radio Sonic*, *Vintage 97/98 Anthology*).

I would like to thank Brian Lam and Blaine Kyllo of Arsenal Pulp Press for their support and their expansive ideas. Thank you also to Lorna Crozier for her master editing and hours of conversation in the garden beside Patrick's pond (with the sometimes broken pump), accompanied by Roxy the cat with nose and ankles like mine.

Thank you to Jann Arden, Leon Brass, Brian Brett, Ron Casat, Isaiah Di Lorenzo, Valerie Fortney, Mattie Gillespie, Anne Green, Martin Guderna, James Keelaghan, Lesa Kirk, Patrick Lane, Joanna McIntyre, Pamela B. McKeown, Sidney Morozoff, Michele Moss, Erin Mouré, Billeh Nickerson, Les Sieminiuk, Hannah Stillwell, Keith Turnbull, Julie Trimingham, Harry Vandervlist, Bob White, Maralyn Wilson, Bill Wilson, and Walter Wittich.

Thank you also to Alberta Theatre Projects and Banff Theatre Arts for playRites Colony '97, The Alberta Foundation for the Arts, The Drunken Poets Society of Calgary, and TheatreSports of Vancouver.

For Sisters
Babz Chula, Trudi Forrest, Donna Miles & Gabrielle Rose
friends
for many years

I love myself when I
am laughing and then again
when I am looking
mean and impressive
– Zora Neale Hurston

DIRECT HIT

YOU'RE MY LIQUOR I JUST WANNA GET PISSED ON YOU

You are my not-so-dry 007
all shook vermouthed and ready to, please
with olive popping pimento
memento mori mento
please, partake through single-malt-soaked lips
and savour 'til dawn
please, affinity 'til dawn
bonded

I'm not an alcoholic
I'm just a thirsty person
addicted to spirits
with triple tongue elixir

one taste start feeling flush
more than buzz
taste two, can't get up off the floor
hammered, almost slurring
what doubles do
three, martini eroto-comatose spinning
weaving into walls, plastered
in a blasted state of libational incitement, please

I handle my liquor
and come with a 3.0 warning
tonight I drink you, drink you
drink you, under the table
over the railing, on the staircase
between the doorways
on the other side of the hallway
in the bathroom on the shiny tiles
on the airplane, in a tree
three sheets . two the wind . tie one on
beautifully – but I never mix
my liquors, I want to get pissed on you
just you

You're my liquor
I just wanna get pissed
on you – over the line

You say
never phone me when you're drunk
I say
never phone me when you're sober
I like it better when you're straight up
not watered down – too much ice

Day blends into night blends into night blends into day

O yes
you're my pisser
I just wanna get licked
on you

—OTTAWA, 1998

A ROOM WITH A WINDOW TO JUMP FROM

I saw Smart in blue
smoke rising
the push on
the kiss in
the door stop pause
the obsession
do you sign your name Assassin
in passion's prepaid suite
the room with a window to jump from
drapes stiff as hospital sheets
losing threads

I saw Smart in blue
card key security
lights throb green alternatively
let me, in a signal of go, in
the door ajar
not far from the flesh
nailed to the hinges by your tongue

I saw Smart in blue
jazz sections
the booth with vinyl music
faux suede over hips
and the lunatic tips

I saw Smart in blue
wax candle I hold to you
under bad paintings screwed to the walls
homicide sex imprints burned into head boards
I hook a chandelier to my big toe
and jump
with a note inscribed on my lick
I've got a crush on you
lock the door
jump on the chenille
cover spread

light your body on fire
we won't sleep through this opening
'cause you place yourself
so perfectly
I always know where you are

—OTTAWA, 1998

SHE AND HER AND YOU AND ME ARE INSEPARABLE

When my love swears that she is made of truth
I do believe her, though I know she lies

—WILLIAM SHAKESPEARE

S.H.E. is me thinking of you/before S.H.E. stopped
having something to lie about/me/to H.E.R./self/to you
S.H.E. takes off all H.E.R. jewellery/on terrace rooftop up there with
jazz/where chimes don't know what to say
soundless blowing down the boulevard/are lyric rays
S.H.E. is up there where a child draws birds into perfect v's
S.H.E. draws you all over/traces you between H.E.R. laugh lines
S.H.E. will draw you/close/super-impose/me/with you/with rays to spare
until S.H.E. smells you/in a hint/half full of desert/me
between juice-filled cacti/spiky on the outside/a café spat
moist of the in/contrast/S.H.E. says/*I can't stand the heat*
horny desert S.H.E./cacti strap themselves on/to the hips of sand
H.E.R. jazz soaked vantage grains/pointed as electric accessories/S.H.E.
no inside jokes/no asides/no stories to remind H.E.R./runway clear
S.H.E. says/*catch the next flight/romance tastes so good/between our shoulders*/on terrace rooftop up there with jazz/S.H.E. wants
more/S.H.E. says/*I want you*/please come closer/to where I lie
let me catch you mid-air/me/without landing/or saying the truth
where the sand horizon meets the desert street lamp/more light
rays of shadow/to trip on/*I'll catch a cab*
won't you come with me tonight/you move me more than
more than/than/more/more/more rays/you/me/moré

—CALGARY, 1998

LEFT

A million miles from mile end
I found a skeleton key in my case
to remind me to turn
or return to you

The ashes of your father
sit restless in the cupboard
and cry out to be scattered or buried–
so does my heart

It's looking for dry land
on this rainy day

—VANCOUVER, 1997

IF YOU GO INSIDE – YOU BETTER HAVE WRITTEN A WILL – 'CAUSE YOU MAY NOT COME OUT ALIVE

White silk slips
all around me
white silk memories
suspended all around me
like movie screens
all around me
white slip movie screens
wearing pictures of my life
all around me
on their midriffs and their breasts and their straps
women I have loved invisible
wearing memories of my life
all around me

On my
white silk slip, my body

Travelling up a steep mountain
one step in front of the other
the edge alluring – a long seduction
blue stars for eyes

I stop
look down
water all around
I'm standing
on the tip of a cliff
shadow turned stone
can't move

Sky so big the clouds are anorexic
standing on the tip of a shale cliff
looking down

Into water, rising
flood water, rising
suffocating the world below
screams muffled in a pillow

Rising
to my own reflection, rising
to my toes
touching toes
and my ankles
up my legs warm enough to melt
balancing on a dissolving grave
water rising

snake charming the charmer
hypnotizing quim into stillness
over my body rising
searching within the curves
shrill end of live-wire nerves
fish belly white belly with slight
rise, nightmare's shivering
verve
nipples holding pearl hard sand
can't move
washed in your baptismal waters
speechless in a chill
dream of swimming – swim of dreaming

Corpses of the dead world
rise up
all around me
an ocean of apostle ghosts
epitaph's jellyfish underwater
without eyes
their nightgown's swell – into mute bells
I can see your face

Ris
ing

through water rising
over my chin
covering my ears
I sink in silence
as a succubus
finger moves deeply
inside me
brings me alive again
makes my hollow bones
feel again
underwater eyelid blur

I climb to the bottom
drag the rope anchored to the sunken world
and pull
the bells ringing

drag the rope anchored to the sunken world
pull
the bells ringing

drag the rope anchored
pull
the bells ringing
the bells ringing
the ringing
the ringing

Under the Galilean moons

—POOLE, 1997

WISHBONE AT TATE

SHE FLOATS IN DARKNESS ON A WOODEN RAFT
IMAGINE HER – WOMAN IN MAN RAY'S
A L'HEURE DE L'OBSERVATOIRE – LES AMOUREUX
SHE FLOATS IN THE DARKNESS OF HER OPIUM SEA –
BELOW LIPS
PENDULUM SWINGS METRONOME – LIGHT LEVITATES – SHADE
SHE CAN'T TELL IF SHE'S MOVED – ALL THE WAVES LOOK
THE SAME
DARKNESS TAKES HER SO FAR INSIDE
SHE SINGS TO HERSELF

I just can't get enough of you
I just can't get enough
I just can't get enough of you
I just can't get enough
trying to fit my heart into the shape of a wishbone

You were born the day of the penetrating gaze
you stretch through my dreams – open scene blaze
here I burn – between destination points
on a sated half-moon night – here I burn
old clock died on the hour – bone fire

SHE THINKS
THERE'S NO SUCH THING AS LIFE
ONLY STONES

I just can't get enough of you
I just can't get enough
I just can't get enough of you
I just can't get enough
trying to fit my heart into the shape of a wishbone

I'm licked by the love of your slide guitar
when longings turn into wind – straining – trying to catch desire
as it lifts in the air – holding – I want you – sound pulling
a long note – swept – trying to hold onto itself - away

Meet me in front of LES HOMMES N'EN SAURONT RIEN
at two o'clock on Tuesday – stop – and let's move
to another savvy corner – behind closed eyes – where no one sees
shed our skin and slink – inside a painting
mix our sweat with pigment upon pigment – hot-blooded strokes
long and silk – not even centuries can come between – our brushes
close to the border of heaven
trying to fit our hearts into the shape of a wishbone

MINUTE HANDS LEFT HANGING
ON THE WALL
LOOKING FOR A TOMBSTONE NAMED REASON
SHE THINKS

I just can't get enough of you
I just can't get enough
I just can't get enough of you
I just can't get enough

—LONDON, 1996

ZIG ZAG LIGHTNING

BUKOWSKI ON THE BLOCK AH-HA

"Peace and quiet are in your future."

—FORTUNE COOKIE

Look, you've got Bukowski's underwear
on display in plexiglass cubes
you've got Bukowski on the rocks, okay
you've got the handkerchief he used to blow his nose
a ripped unwashed undershirt
petrified
in a mock plexiglassed closet, without doors
you've got his socks
his empty shoes
just to set the mood of streets well-tread
not a word that he said
not a word that he said
"there is hardly anything as sad as a run-over cat"

You've got his pastel plaid arrow
shirt and baby blue jacket
he wore to the races – shoulda left no traces!
you've got his driver's licence, his un-
spent money, a bottle opener, his unsmoked cigar
you've even got his unused band-aid on display
like he planned his scars in advance

Come on!
where are the rejection letters that said he stepped over the line
the toilet where he puked
his big yellow cat
the hopeless nights
classical music on the radio
and another bottle of plonk
where's the well-drunk wine?

Bukowski's licking cunt he's gonna share chicken and coleslaw with later!
Blam Wham!
that's when my rant
hit the Flitcroft cobblestones
hard
slide it in
slide it out – blow the bard
that's when I got tossed from the "American Realist" show
now you see it
now you don't
please, adjust clothing
before leaving – face your cards
Bukowski's life reduced to t-shirt sales
and what would he say?

ching ching
outside my hotel window
one whore screams at another
you fucked my fuck you fuckin' fuck!
ha

ching ching
in a doorway a fifteen-year-old
with a needle between her teeth hisses
kiss and a fix
kiss and a fix
for a fiver
ha

ching ching
and O, Imperial does mean something
'cause in wine
size does matter

I say
wacko scumsucker looking for a scab

In the gallery down on Flitcroft Street
you watch your wallet
close as a second skin
and what can I say?
at St. Paul's it costs four quid to pray
and there's no end to my
generosity

Bukowski thought balling was "making it"
and a low-rent brand of romance
BUKowski on the block ah-ha
is irony the language of slaves?

—LONDON, 1996

O HAIL THEE MIGHTY CABBY

Hail cab O holy light blinking
beacon on a broken night CABBY
hail to thee mine chariot
into the San Francisco night
O mighty one, blinking cab
holy light coming toward me on this broken night
unforgiving and destructive
hail to thee, blithe spirit
bird thou never wert
hail O thee for me
radiant illuminatrix in all beings over there
circle whose circumference is nowhere
and whose centre is everywhere
pick me up and take me into the broken night
and fix it, and fix it
and fix it, and fix it
what is a broken night?
down the crazy inclines of the cities
spilling sight
twelve gold moons are glowing in the heat of holy love
chariot driving CABBY
take me
pick me up
I said *take me*, I said *pick me up*
take me I'm yours
O mighty infinite CABBY
pick me up and take me where I'm going
I'm close enough to the tenderloin to get marinated
I said, *I'm close enough to the tenderloin to get marinated*
I said, *I'm close enough to the tenderloin to get marinated*
and on this crazy heat holy night you're being serenaded
by me, holy night light CABBY
pull over to the curb of me sweet sideswiper of the supreme
and pick me up and meter me
and meter me
and meter me
O bliss CABBY

holy light blinking *Signum dei*
beacon on a broken night
pray I, to thee, mine creator chariot guide
mine blinking benevolent mighty righteous-one cosmic ride
hail O thee for me divine deity
and take me into the night my blinking baby
and drive me home
and drive me home
and drive me all the way home
through the broken night
O holy love beacon blinking one!

—SAN FRANCISCO, 1997

STAYING AT THE BALMORAL HOTEL

for Pamela B. McKeown

Staying at the Balmoral Hotel
residue 'round the corner from residence
hidden costs under-stone – scramble out of light
admit one – defenestrate delusion – no sun
in this city *where hearts get left behind*
a cloud's cape filled with mistful thinking
a dream to dance flamenco – she did her hair up everyday
with pins and spray – with polished shoes she stepped through
her fourth-story window pane – for the thrill
she jumped – from the frame – yelling
I'm only a picture – my glass won't break today
there's a stain where she used to hang
in the pink room with the brick wall view
no escape – no outside world to wonder on
just the keys to an inner city dive that won't supply towels
she called home – removed her make-up and wound her alarm
every night – afterhours it's always the same
what's the cover, Mister?

A clapboard sign in Chinatown reads:
Who-Creates-Injustice?

Staying at the Balmoral Hotel
Alfred Jarry Mardi Gras in the lobby
pay phone out-of-order – lost 25 sense – calling help
side-show of walkie talkies arrive with cherries screaming
ask the X-con-man-ager why he left Montana
he says, *went there to live my life, but it didn't work*
derelict TV snowing in the corner – dying for a channel change
double exposure – this world and the next
crowd gathers spectacle – cops try to control – questions – remote
ferris wheel music – blaring on their radios
someone says, *who gets her loveseat?*
fashion junkies – payin' their dues for the chunkiest shoes
bankrolled by nowhere jobs – turn up – with the coolest blues

to say *cheese* in drycleaned monkey suits – *heard someone died here*
mind if we take a few shots – direct hit – in Frisco-town
first church of the last laugh – the longest yard – the highest hill
the tallest bridge – the biggest heart
to jump from – choose your day

Staying at the Balmoral Hotel
I'm only a picture – my glass won't break today
what's the cover, Mister?
who-creates-injustice?
went there to live my life, but it didn't work
who gets her loveseat?
cheese
heard someone died here
mind if we take a few shots

in this heat
it's a damn breeding ground
gotta watch yourself

—SAN FRANCISCO, 1998

THE NEW YORK WALDORF ELEVATOR GENIE BITCH

the doors open – and there she is
a goddamned Genie
standing in the elevator at The Waldorf in New York City
all dressed up with perfect eyeliner and a funky hat
waiting for me like I just rubbed something
or something

I get on – doors close – start wishing
she ignores me like I'm invisible
or crazy or panhandling or coming on

I think, I thought Genies were beyond that
I think, I thought they spoke all dialects of all languages
to all people everywhere without prejudice
I think, I thought they were open-minded liberalists
I mean, they live in bottles
for Christ's sake, who are they to judge?

feel like I've wasted a wish
like I've been cheated out of my magic penny
standing at the well with my eyes closed
like the wind blew my party candles out
like the clown didn't show up
feel like, a little hurt, let down

the New York Waldorf elevator Genie
just stands there like an over-dressed stiff
ignoring my wishes like they might go away

bing
the doors open – she gets off

I mean
why is she riding an elevator in the first place?
doesn't she know Genies can fold their arms
and with a nod of their head
a bat of their eye, a twitch of their nose

split, in a puff of smoke to wherever they want
doesn't she know Genies don't need airplane tickets?

maybe she's a Genie in training
I don't know
but the next night I'm dancing at The Studio
and there she is
The New York Waldorf elevator Genie Bitch
there she is, beside me, doin' the hustle
she gives me a dirty look
so I know she knows who I am
The New York Waldorf elevator Genie Bitch
so I give her one back, with a human twist
long and dirty and cruel

we're even
with one look
I let her know that I know that she's not a real Genie
that she's not makin' anyone's wishes come true
this day or even someday soon
she's a fake, pretender, poser, wanna-be, Genie bitch

I blow her cover
tell the guy dancing beside me in the gold lamé jock strap
with the roller skates that light up when he twirls
that she's not a real Genie
that she only wishes she were a real Genie
that she's a wanna-be Genie bitch
who's never seen the inside of any bottle

and he says
don't worry darlin'
I only watch I DREAM OF JEANNIE
'cause I'm in love with the astronaut

and as we dance
I hope my defamatory thoughts
don't spring from my mind
and hit the New York Waldorf elevator Genie Bitch
in her well-lined eye
'cause she'll sue
I can grant you that much

—BANFF, 1997

FAST FOR-WORDS

I said
listen you little prick
I'm not selling out
I'm making a fucking living
in a right-wing western town
that would persecute me
for not carrying an inscribed mother-of-pearl handled
pistol in my briefcase

I said
I'm making a living
as an independent artist
you know how hard that is, bell boy?
I know
you've heard it all before
donkey dink
you've got a roomless alternative press
that sleeps when it wants to screw
who knew?

fast for-words before I fuck you
selling out? – replay
man, have you got any idea where I've been . . . living
got any idea how I've made one?
or does it scare ya, never-left-Calgary homeboy town?
guess in your eyes it would be okay
if I was walking the streets
if I was turning a few artistic tricks
juggling my cunt for a living
suppose that would be okay with you
then you'd never accuse me of selling out –
so I'm making a living
hate to break it to ya, but the work has grit
you can take the girl outta the gutter
can't take the curb outta the girl . . . shit
do you know how many times I've been banned, prick boy?

do you know how many times I've been forced to
sit on the face of revulsion
for less than a day's salary
how much do you make in your safe little pretty job, blow boy
there is no alternative
alternative to what?
looks like the only person that's sitting on the fence
between the two cheeks of my art, is you
asshole
so
suck my dick
even if I don't
have one

if you really are the "alternative" voice of Calgary
chicken shit
print this

—CALGARY, 1998

THIS POEM IS TO BE READ OUT LOUD

SLEEPING IN THE AIR

has always been impossible for me
I'm afraid I'll start drooling, I'll be
the kid that crammed the whole box of Smarties into her mouth
red, green, yellow, brown – leaking out the sides

Sleeping in the air

has always been impossible for me
I might dream we're about to crash
we're going down – everyone screaming
on a "cheep" no-points flight
the bird loses part of its wing over France
I release the life jacket below my seat – start screaming
stay calm, we're going to land in the ocean, the pilot's dying of food poisoning but the hijacker's going to land this thing
wonder what happens to the pieces of the bird that fly off
over France?

Sleeping in the air

has always been impossible for me
I'm afraid I'll start sleepwalking towards the bathroom
break the law in the lavatory, light up a cigarette
set off the smoke detector
I throw the cigarettes in the toilet, pretend to be peeing
just as the flight police knock down the bathroom door
the toilet explodes – sucks me out into the sky
another no-points flight

Sleeping in the air

has always been impossible for me
I'll start playing with myself
masturbate under the blanket like a sex-crazed badger
dream the person next to me is my long-distance lover
start having phone sex, rip off my clothes
rub myself against the arm rest yelling *harder, harder*

my inflatable pillow gets punctured, starts flying around
like an out-of-control balloon, my head still attached to it
jets around the plane expelling belligerent fart sounds
like a deflating female John the Baptist on a flying platter-pillow
that lands in the centre of a crackdown on passenger abuse
in the air rage my head receives a yellow card
after biting the flight attendant
yelling obscenities and spitting on the food cart
puts a whole new spin on the mile high club
the flight attendant starts chasing
my soon-to-be-imprisoned flying head, yelling
if you like chicken I suggest you have the fish
if you like fish I suggest you have the chicken

Sleeping in the air

has always been impossible for me

—IN THE AIR, OVER THE ROCKIES, 1998

SHE DOESN'T KNOW I'M A DOG

"One could almost claim it is the dog who makes us human."
—MARJORIE GARBER

I've always related to Dogs, in a special way
like I have some secret knowledge, howling
and guarding

Canus Corpa Transmuto
I'm a Dog! A She-Dog/en français/She-Dog chien
only speak French
francophone/She-Dog chien
a Dober-Woman-Pincer/She-Dog chien
only wear black/coats
love me/love me/love me

It started at birth
born the year of the Dog
O yes/born She-Dog chien/the year of the Dog
in the flesh/in the fur
Dog
I'll never tell my Dog age

I'll be at a party and someone'll ask
if you were an animal, what kind would it be?
and I'll answer Dog/She-Dog chien
I only speak French
and then they say
if you're a Dog, what kind?
and I say
don't mince with me, be aware
I'm a Dober-Woman-Pincer/I glare
no roll over play dead, beg for milk bones or fetching balls
for this cunning canine, no stupid Dog tricks
believe me, you don't want to see my other side, ha
my bark's not bigger than my bite
at the party they laugh/they don't want to know the truth
I don't blame them

Canus Corpa Transmuto
I'm a Dog! A She-Dog/en français/She-Dog chien
only speak French
francophone/She-Dog chien
a Dober-Woman-Pincer/She-Dog chien
only wear black/coats
love me/love me/love me

I've always liked rhinestone chokers
being petted
a one-room house of my own
being chained to a spike, escapes into night
over the fence in one clean leap, I'm down the alley
fuck 'em I'm free
never been caught, never been to the pound

Doggie shake a paw

I love scaring people at the front door
one look at me and they run
they don't know what to do when I start
humping their legs

I love panting
'specially on a hot day, tongue out, breathing hard
don't even need a reason

I've always liked licking myself

I've been a lucky Dog
liked going out/putting myself on/putting on the Dog
sniffing around
I'm a dish of a Dog – I got great Doggie style
watch what you're saying above my back
I can hear better than you

Can't even see a fire hydrant
without my hairs standing on end
it makes me nervous

this uncontrollable urge to sniff
God, I should carry extra oxygen in my cat-fur purse

Sometimes I have dreams of Dober-Men-Pincers
behind me, sniffing my butt
they know
I've gotten in touch with my inner
B.I.T.C.H.
Beautiful / Intelligent / Talented / Clairvoyant / Horny
Bitch – bitchy bitch

I always turn around three times before I lie down
on the floor to sleep
that's where I explore, multiple Dog dream dimension
I remember once, on the radio, talking dirty, I swore
and Daddy Doggie tore into me
saying
you dragged the family name across the carpet
like an old Dog
And I said
Of course I did, Daddy, I'm a Dog
but not so old

Canus Corpa Transmuto
And I'm Dog!/A She-Dog
A Dober-Woman-Pincer Dog/She-Dog chien

I chase tail
bark at the moon when it hits the horizon
'cause it's in my blood

I'll test you
growl through my teeth, snap and froth a little
for the challenge
if you stand up to me, human bites Dog
I know I can respect you, for life
really, down deep, I'm a healer not a herder

O and I love chasing rabbits
men in uniforms I cannot resist
cops, meter readers, firemen, gas jockeys
airline pilots, and mailmen drive me nuts
outta my mind,
anything as long as it looks official
I will even chase and threaten
Maytag repairmen/sniff/sniff/sniff

I will chew anything
just for the heck of it

Canus Corpa Transmuto
And I'm a Dog!

Next time I'm at a wedding
and someone's buggin' me to dance
I'll say
If we don't do the dirty dog
I've got two left feet

If I love you I'll wag my tail
yes, it's small
when they say size matters
they're not talking about wagging it

Beware of Dog – those signs hurt my feelings
always hoping they're dyslexic

Call me a Dog
I love it when you say "come"

—HALIFAX, 1996

M.I.-5 SPY

arrive exactly
on the first of seven bells – never arrive late for a spy
feel her eyeball pierce through the peephole, sting
door haunted by its own safety
devices – she invites me in – air-raid warning

the flat's a war zone
seventy-five years of death-mess – basement bunker, suite
throw rugs wrinkling trenches into timeworn floors
exponential piles of life debris – growing – feel them – growing
wars
congregating for centuries
before expi-ry dates
dust from the Roman invasion
buried there
what's buried there
we sit down, she asks what I write
damn
hell bursts out of the cracks – wall snakes with a hiss
the collector

I say
sex and death

bombs away
her cane waves ballistic S.O.S.s
"help" – stolen purses at Tesco's
Kali venom flares into a hissy-fit mushroom
around her eighty-year head
no two – bones about it – three
firing squad bullet towards me in slow-mo
no blindfold, see it coming just before it strikes

if she weren't so old, I'd tell her to "fuck off"
instantly – under attack skyrocketing into
my only defence – humour – not working
leg-hold trapped

she says
never talk about sex or money

I say
yeah right, never talk about religion, politics, movies or books

my comment lodges my bullet deeper, shite!
she carves a placemat-sized rectangle
in the ceiling-high rubble of newspapers and junk
places my dog dish on the mat in front of me
three inches thick in age-old grease and scum
pile of half-cooked sauceless spaghetti plunked on top
yum

this looks delicious!

Canadian decorum kicks in
I eat off the top of the noodles
don't eat the noodles that touch the scummy plate
pretend to be full

yum, thank you, Mrs. Merse, delicious!

she starts her banter about starvation

I say
Suffering Succotash

we're off to the landmine races
if I'd suffered like she and so many others had suffered
I would've eaten my own plate . . .
. . . and part of your fork . . .
. . . I wouldn't be making wisecracks about some stupid American cartoon
I bite my tongue

It just gets worse and worse with Mrs. Merse

she says
if you have to write about sex obviously you've never starved

I say
no, if I write about it, obviously I'm not getting any

what do you write about sex, anyway?

I say
ecstasis, erotica – picture a woman's face while she's having an orgasm
open to light body curves before it arches
to an appoint-
meant for mouth
shaking into the private cosmos, years pass over her face
travelling throughout the intimate place of herself

disgusting

I think the orgasm's beautiful

what do you mean?
sex is only to create children

I don't need a man to have an orgasm
I can have an orgasm walking down the street
or sitting on a stone

you're disgusting

with all due respect I don't think so

there are only two subjects to write about in life, thirst and hunger

beady-eyed X-M.I.-5 spy, woman
who abused you at your gravesite?
who looked down your hole and spat?

people with AIDS deserve to die, because they had sex for pleasure

Mrs. Merse
you don't have to wear leather
you've become your own enemy
your own torturer
beady-eyed X-M.I.-5 spy
Nazi woman

notice what this is about

—LONDON, 1996

THE SWEET TASTE OF LIGHTNING

"Warning: never leave burning candle unattended."

—A. COSTCO

She had a house full of candles
she never burned

lightning struck the world white
crashed the roof – sky hitting

tones of darkness – slam
she wasn't wearing her underwire bra

it flew through the veins of her house
hit the heart – blew everything out

all the appliances spoke at once
in magnetic tongues

the blind dog barked – snapped at the air
ran into furniture

all the mirrors flashed black
black mirrors – she couldn't see herself

everything was running
away from her, singed

electric candy swirled on her tongue
the sweet taste of lightning

—CALGARY, 1998

LIFE BOLT

GINSBERG'S GONE GONE GONE

but not so far away
that we can't taste him in the jism of our memory
that we can't touch him in the fuck of his words
that we can't feel him, fetal
ever-trembling in an after-sex chill
snapping pictures
standing at the door opening to the other side
his body's a curling mandala
opening wide, so he can ecstasis us
like a crazy man
O yes O yes

Ginsberg's gone gone gone
but not so far away from Naropa
that dharma desert day when he said
keep on going
look for epiphanies in your madness
he said
keep on going
crazy
O yes O yes

Ginsberg's gone gone gone
but not so far away
from the archive viewing room that stoned desert day
where I was watching an aged video
a cutting clip with Jack Kerouac raving angry beat
denouncing Ginsberg and what he called the beat elite
and the camera left high Jack
scanned the audience and tracked Ginsberg young and soundless
sitting there in the audience being panned by his old friend Jack
the angry dead beat caught with his drunken shorts down

Jack went off
he went off
Jack went way-off-track
in fact, he completely fuckin' derailed

there on the video
Ginsberg didn't even react
by beat
by beat

in real time Ginsberg comes to the door
peeks in, sees I'm watching him
as a much younger man
freezes
says
may I join you?
I say
please
I mean why not, it's Ginsberg for Christ's sake

he sits down beside me and I watch what he sees
on the video that day
I see him drift away from himself
audience to audience caught on tape
escape in and out of himself
fall into that crazy crack that poets talk about
I view him sitting in symbols
    in well-read rooms
    his black and white photos
    finger bells punctuate sound
I see a come shot of wrist-locked passion
    caught on a paper sheet
I see him in protest
    sitting on the rails
    cross-legged between ties
I see his love for Cody muse
    hear him sigh when Cody dies
I see him fall to his knees
    cock his thought gun in the kitchen
    swing off the branches of beautiful young boys
    howl and spit at half-moon skies
    Blake whirling 'round in prayer
I see a constant discovery of everything
    everywhere, in song

And I see an asshole misogynist
    who never got over his mother

and then
I watch him come back
to the place where he keeps the voice of Kerouac
his friend
the man he loved
alive

and in that moment time joins itself
between the man I saw
and the man I'm seeing
and we're holding hands
gliding in and out of time
in the Buddhist desert
sand to sand
o yes

Ginsberg saw with his soul
stretched out wide
yeah
I say
goodbye
see you tomorrow
all that remains of this morning
is you leaving

—SEATTLE, 1997

AVUNCULAR

when he ski-doo'ed he really ski-doo'ed

that's what they said about my uncle when he died

and well, he ski-doo'ed, he ski-diddled,
he ski-doddled, he ski-daddled

he ski-died
before his time

INCH-BY-INCH

He died inch-by-inch
    I watched him die by the inch
    in the end he didn't remember his name

The Alzheimer's made him not know things
    crazy
    or he'd know half-things
    he'd put the half-things he'd know
    together with the half-things he'd lost
    and we'd end up with another disaster

O
    some of the things he did were really funny

One day
    when I was out getting groceries
    he decides he's going to do a little gardening
    incredible
    he always hated gardening
    couldn't get him to pick a flower

    I go out and he decides to do some gardening
    when I come back all hell's broken loose

He had the lawn mower inside the house
    he was mowing the living room carpet
    there he was
    just mowing our good Persian rug
    with this big fat smile across his face
            like it was the happiest moment of his life
            like he'd just won the lottery or something –
            clouds of smoke everywhere

I don't know if he was vacuuming the lawn
    or mowing the carpets!

He died by the inch
    I watched him die by the inch
    in the end he didn't remember his name

I had to place him in high maintenance
    'cause I just couldn't do it all anymore
    then I get a call from the hospital
    saying there's nothing more they can do with him
    he needed too much care
    for the hospital

Where was he supposed to go
    dying by the inch

I was beside myself
    couldn't take it – broke down

I asked if there was anything they could do
    anything
    and the nurse says
    do you have a briefcase of his?

Yes

Bring it tomorrow

So I go back the next day with his briefcase
    the nurses and doctors
    were telling him all morning
    he had a lunch meeting
        sort of puffing him up
        making his day feel important

At lunch they got him dressed
    they gave him his briefcase
    and they took him for lunch

Well
    he was just beaming like a big old toad
    smiling and nodding

The next day
when we were leaving the hospital
the nurse called out
Stew, you forgot your briefcase
and he turned around
and he just beamed again

I went back and got it

That day he recognized his name
he inched backwards
and for an instant he was him

He died by the inch
I watched him die by the inch
he didn't remember his name
he didn't know who I was

—PORTLAND, 1997

HE WENT BY JOE

and you are here with me
buffalo ghost in foothills
an oldness on my lips
a bend in a tree
by the river the cool water
on a moon-full night

and you are here with me
running with the children in moccasins
watching PowWow dancers
your name would have been Joe
the light shadows, you know
you never got to kick me
never heard your heart

and you are here with me
as grave robbers dig with their hands
and shade remembers your name
the river carries us along
she carries us along
the slippery stones of her skin

and you are here with me
Head-Smashed-In Buffalo Jump
you are here with me
watching centuries ease into twilight
you are here
under branches between pines

how old would you be?
at this gathering under blue water skies
how old would you be?
in this joy I see clear through
to the bottom
how old would you be?
in this pond full of sky

this is no prayer
just a little song that keeps singing
you are here

—HEAD-SMASHED-IN BUFFALO JUMP, 1997

FAMOUS LAST WORDS

I

Swearing by accident – accidentally
cursing ourselves into death
seven years for a broken mirror

did the Darwin Award drunken guy
yell *Fuck* as he flew off the cliff?
did his high-alcohol-level friend
yell *Fuck* when the car exploded?
did the pissed party-joke guy who threw himself
at the plateglass window to prove it wouldn't break
yell *Fuck* as he started to fly
towards becoming an outline
on the ground?

II

With mirrors breaking
it is between the hand and the floor
that the luck is lost

Two women
come falling down
the stone stone stairs of Eden
two women
come spilling down – from the top
of Eden – down the stone stone stairs
tumbling down toppling
two women Eden
down come turning
ball lightning rolling
from the top blurring
come – two fall downing
stone stair turning
not faking falling
coming to – while turning
stair stoning two women falling
down turning

through shadows
fall breaking
Eden topping
after
too
much
Sake
and
too
little
fish

One woman
heavier than the other
with crutches
already airborne broken
leg still plastered
casting lost balance
comes soaring – from the tip toppling
second women tries to catch her
mid-air already spilling
lost in balance from the top
toppling
two women
down

Two women
one uglier than the other
falling down
the stone stone stairs
ripped
two women
reflecting – in air
falling down stone stairs
had enough air time
zero to sixty
to say their famous last words
to each other

fuck
said one woman

fuck
said the second

fuck
said the first
turning in the second's bony arms

fuck
said the second
as they hit

Two women – bust broken
stopped
with four fucks and stone
between them

III

Upon reflection

A woman's hand gets caught
in the prop of a plane
ending it while starting it
swearing in and out

The words on her gravestone read:
last word
fuck

How many people's last words were . . . ?

—SEATTLE, 1997

BALL LIGHTNING

NAILS AND LASHES

Negative testing with positive results

one – two – three testing

positive with negative results

not again – you're not sick again

you're a million dollar baby

a line to the fault–

ghosting over Rainforest river

don't die of denial – Cha-cha-la

don't die of denial

live again with bangles flying all-jangle

gypsy flare – head dashing – daring eyes

wild dance for a walk – hypnotize – with snappy fire-steps

in crazy white go-go boots with fringe

a snazzy style – only you

black hair and major jazz earrings sculpting

the well-rounded curves of your face

you always arrived with home-baked bread

gifts for the girls

The Canasta Club – lists and lists of wishes

you were always the good one, for Christ's sake

the one who did everything right

in your big hats, with your brightly painted toenails

negative thinking from positive results

tested – I don't want you to die

in your vaulted skylight living room

trees rooted in massive clay pots of earth

shrunk beaten into a corner

won't be the only mourner

over-grown and under-watered

crinkled curled and ready to crack

your perfume was always the strong kind

Cha-cha-la – waves come in grief

lying in a dying house

untended music searching

notes to an uneven score

slam went time, crash went the door

I said

Cha-cha-la, what a great place to live

You said

yes I've been very lucky

as if . . . your ticket had been drawn

as if . . . you'd worn a rubber

as if . . . you had a full house

no insult begins more difficult than a positive result

tested – stuck by a safety pin

it might go away, I don't have it, it might go away

I locate you in your dementia

when you forget – the moment before a moment ago/before

cutting split ends off

intoxicated full moon

look alive

for the picture and the page

it won't go away

but you will

you will

when someone you love dies

do you leave them in your phone book

so you can always stay in touch?

—VICTORIA, 1998

THE DE SADE FAMILY ESCAPES SALTANA RESEARCH SITE AND THEY MOVE IN NEXT DOOR

for Jessica Vidican-Neisius

No one else would . . .
. . . after the murders

Not certain what possessed me
  not exactly sure what the lure
  something, something, made me cross that solid yellow line
  that usually defines those six degrees of precious separation

With monomaniacal anticipation I went to say *Hi*
To my new narcoleptic neighbours

No one else would . . .
. . . after the murders

There's Mother un-nerving neighbour
  the size of a candy bar machine
  with pencil thin lips and a three-tooth smile
  a well-armoured oral compulsive
  bag of chips in her mouth all the while – crunching
    always followed by a slurping sound
    no underwear – drip marks on the floor
    catch the occasional off-putting flash
    the periodical whiff, what panties are for

There's Father un-nerving neighbour
  with vice-grip beer-bottle-opening eye sockets
  and a mind revolutionary as the rotary dial
  he washes his hands in petrol before dinner
  and smells Mr. Gasoline diesel vile
    morning after a hard night drinking
    a cartoon stream of bile oozes from their house
    into the street
    nobody dares step outside – 'til the sun burns it off a little

And then there's five-year-old Warren Shamus
doesn't take long for Warren Shamus to get famous
Dennis the Menace on masochist steroids
at five he burgles the block
with Mummy De Sade killer nail file
he rubs his eyes with sandy hands, says
I'm sorry, take me to trial
so help me God – he never returns the goods, instead
he builds a beratement dungeon in the basement
invites the 'hood kids for an S&M birthday bash
what's more
he makes them don leather masks – pins them to the floor
calls them donkeys
makes them eat chocolate cake through their noses
leather, spikes, everything nice he-ha hard-core

And O
there's baby un-nerving neighbour
the vibrating fledgling boy – who everyone feels sorry for
his sole purpose in life, it would seem
is to serve as Warren Shamus' Tonka toy

Which came first, I don't know who to blame
is it the bilbosy chains they use to restrain
Warren Shamus to the living room chair?
is it the quadruple espresso shooters that make him bizarre?
or the lack of Mummy De Sade's underwear?
Warren Shamus, Warren Shamus, one more time and you're going to your chastise chair

Sitting in the De Sade discipline family kitchen
high octane dungeon
something strikes me as odd
Mother un-nerving neighbour asks Warren Shamus
in a hung-over voice between slurping and crunches
would you like a refill, dear?
Warren Shamus holds up his Mickey Mouse cup
confident as a lifelong trucker on an all-night haul
gimme another hit of velocity, Mummy

Mother un-nerving neighbour says
now don't you swig, I want you to sip
Warren Shamus says
you're not the boss'a me
she laughs
and what about you, baby, you want some more Jitter-juice?
baby holds up his Little Mermaid cup
Mother says
look, baby wants more coffee, isn't that the cutest thing

A couple of weeks ago
his parents are in the front of the house
drinking brews
I catch Warren Shamus playing HAMMER HEAD
with baby De Sade
in the rear of the house

Warren Shamus
is following baby crawling sweet pea up the back stairs
Warren Shamus
is pounding a hammer alternatively on either side of baby's head
on the right side
thud
on the left side
thud
on the right side
thud
on the left side
thud
the old house shakes – I want to stay on his good side
things blow off their shelves – his good side
I'm afraid to stop him – both sides bad for the baby
I want to stay on his good side – whatever that is
don't say anything
run away before he catches me catching him – and hide

Actually they were very good neighbours
didn't mind if we played our stereo loud

—SEATTLE, 1998

that crazy cat

"there is hardly anything as sad as a run-over cat"
—CHARLES BUKOWSKI

hey, remember that poor freaky cat

four legs on the ground
four legs on its back
that poor freaky eight-legged cat

scared the living daylights out of me
always playing in lightning
that's what they said those who'd seen it

everyone in town talking about that cat

I got up extra early
combed the streets looking for
that bloody freak cat

finally found it
eight legs
just like everyone said

it was scouring alleys looking for food
'cause no one would get near it
smelled noxious in the morning burn
between the silver cans, skulking

and then it came out
everyone in town was talking about it
that Marty kid
skinned one cat
and glued it onto the back of another

he was sort of looked on
like some kind of hero
Marty the modern-day-cat-skinning hero

everyone poking fun
at him "shame, shame"
and at the same time they'd be laughing
under their cruel, fucked-up
Christ loving breath

everyone in town talking about that crazy cat

—BANFF, 1998

BUT THE SEX WAS GOOD

received a scorpion/registered/had to sign for the sting
as if I hadn't paid enough already
                                        but the sex was good
everything moved in straight lines
no room for chance/instinct/no twist in perception
no maps to an unknown city/just land mines/and flowers
                                        but the sex was good
seduction to sedation/scorpion stings when it's scared
doors slam/plates smash/fists pound/humanity bared
you scream/*I just wanna kick your head in*
you inhale me like I'm your last cigarette 'til I can't breathe/I'm numb
                                        but the sex was good
no pleasure dots to connect/paradise bulldozed
caught an air bound ghetto blaster with an eluding head
talk about seeing stars
                                        but the sex was good
according to the Times/the beverage most often requested on death row is
Coca Cola/the real thing/buy an all-nite drugstore on the skids
ya gotta expect to meet the bugs/older than the serpent
get up or I'll kill you/but I'm already dead/lovemaking on an electric
bed/stone garden erected and engraved/cost me an arm and a leg/static
                                        the sex was good but
high velocity bodies/cloud-to-cloud discharge/cause of
radiation/unknown
you take another smoke beer toke another scotch/blank out
scream prisoner/*don't turn your back to me when you sleep*/you say
                                        but was the sex good
if we were snakes/you would have put my head in your mouth
and eaten me whole/I request a final drink/air
night sticks to day/and stones/and broken bones
you say you've lived in my shadow long enough/I try yours
there isn't one/you sting yourself
though I'm the one who paid/the scorpian registered in my name

—LONDON, 1996

ZEBRA FACES OF MEN WHO HAVE ESCAPED FROM THE ZOO

Zebra faces of men who escaped from the zoo
could kill
they could kill you

He slipped a message underneath her door
on a flattened Tampax box
which read
I'm coming back for you
she called the cops
she waited for them to arrive
there was nothing they could do

There is no such thing as a restraining order
there is only a gun
that can kill

Zebra faces of men who have escaped from the zoo

Had she forgotten to turn off the oven?
she made lemon pie that day
she rose from bed to check
she turned and saw a shadow
moving outside her kitchen window
it was a man trying to break and enter
she tip-toed back to her bedroom
called 911
and she waited
she described things to the woman
on the other end of the line
he went crack-falling
fell into the crack of the city
there were no helicopters
no search light

There is no such thing as a restraining order
    there is only a gun
    that could kill

Zebra faces of men who escaped from the zoo
    she received a scented envelope stamped
    gone with the wind
    it was fall
    she didn't recognize her stalker's hand
    when she opened the letter
    breeze through the bars
    leaves crunch underfoot
    no advice could relieve the fear
    the years she lived with guard dogs, with eyes

The things you lose in life:
    your virginity
    your mind
    your car keys
    and your breath

She found a drill bit
    three feet long
    used to open the ground
    she went home and scribed
    I love you
    on the metal staff in gold letters
    she placed it in the ready position
    and she waited for beauty to begin again

—BANFF, 1997

HE WAS A HOTHEAD

LIGHTS UP ON AN OVERSIZED WOOD FRAME
SUPPORTING A LONG STRING OF WOODEN WINDCHIMES
(MAORI STYLE) – ALMOST PADDLES
THE WIND GENTLY BLOWS THE WOODEN CHIMES –
AN UNDERSCORE
WOMAN RISES OUT OF THE GROUND IN A FULL-LENGTH
LIGHT 30S SLIP
ALMOST AS IF SHE WERE RISING FROM A GRAVE
A CLEAR SKY IS PROJECTED ONTO HER SLIP
SHE ADDRESSES THE AUDIENCE DIRECTLY –
WIND MOVES THE SLIP-SKY

He was a hothead, that morning you could smell his storm brewing. You could smell his storm blow in from the north, brewing and burning. He was a hothead, and he was on fire, that morning.

I was old enough to read the signs, but too young to see the traffic coming, that morning.

I went to visit Deb and Jack. You remember Deb and Jack, we stayed with them when we went skiing that time in Whitewater, 'member? Anyway, Deb and I went out for a few cocktails after she finished work, hadn't seen each other for months so we were blah blah blah, got home around ten, by that time Jack's steaming. Hothead fuming. Strike the steam clock hour, steaming, hothead fuming.

Read the signs, didn't see the traffic coming.

Next morning I come downstairs and Deb's locked in the bathroom screaming blue murder. Jack's trying to break down the bathroom door with a pitchfork, and their two-year-old's going ballistic in his highchair. Great, one happy, well-adjusted family.

THE SKY PROJECTED ON HER SLIP TURNS TO STORM CLOUDS

Then SNAP Bam!
    mountains on the move.
SNAP Bam!

and I'm in one of those heightened states,
where I could lift a fucking truck with my little finger.

SNAP Bam!

and I'm in between them,
"Stop, for God's sake! For God's sake! Stop! Stop! Before someone gets hurt! Before someone gets hurt!"

Then SNAP.

And it's all over, like it didn't exist, and we're sittin' there at the kitchen table having morning coffee. Sittin' there in the kitchen having morning fucking coffee, acting like nothing happened.

O no, that wasn't Jack trying to break down the bathroom door to murder his wife just now. No, no, God, no. It was a rehearsal for a home and garden show. Yeah, yeah, that's what it was, a fucking home and garden show.

And I'm wondering how many times she's hit the snooze button. How many time's she's hit the snooze button, the snooze button. Wonder if she'll ever wake up. Wonder how many time's she won't wake up, wake-up, wake-up.

It's hard to wake up, when you don't know you're asleep.

Hard to go to sleep, when your bed's on fire. Ha.

So we're sitting there pretendin' nothing happened over morning coffee, then Deb goes off to work, and I'm left sitting alone with Mr. Slow Burn. Left having morning coffee with Alan fucking Bates.

Didn't see the traffic coming, deny, deny, deny.

I go upstairs and have a shower, come back to my room, and there he is sitting there like a bloody hitman, waiting for me.

if you don't mind I have to get changed

you don't have to get changed, he growls

WHITE SLIPS BEGIN FILLING THE SPACE
PROJECTED STORM CLOUDS TURN TO LIGHTNING STRIKES
HORRIFIC SLASHES RIPPING ACROSS HER BODY
AND THE OTHER HANGING SLIPS

SNAP
my head's snapped back
SNAP
caught by my hair
SNAP
pushed from behind
SNAP
he's the bank robber and I'm the body
SNAP
he's using me as his shield
SNAP
to stop the bullets, swat team
SNAP
his body's hard against my back
SNAP
down the exploding hallway
SNAP
the hallway streaks
SNAP
pull away animal wild
SNAP
tightens grip dog yank bone
SNAP
into custody's blur
SNAP
thrown across room
SNAP
hand across face

SNAP

thrown against bed

bitch

THE WIND BLOWS HARDER AGAINST THE WOODEN CHIMES

White towel dropped cover, torn naked. Try to kick the fucker in the crotch. Slapping sound coming from my body. He's undoing his fly. His eyes are pitchfork prongs.

don't be afraid

Try to escape through the door's distant frame. Green carpet face-to-face. Slapping sound on back, past pain. Pushing inside me stings, doing hard time. Claw, claw my way away. Crawl, claw my way away. Green claw my way away. Him riding my back like a decapitated prayer. Body turn flap Jack, blinded by a back hand to the face. Back hand to the face. Back hand to the face. Back hand to the face. Cut to smithereens.

Dark stains shoot holes in my head. And I hear myself scream, "Fuck me! Fuck me harder! Fuck me harder! Harder fuck me! Fuck me! Fuck me! Is that all you got, fucker?!" Remember my face from the outside, dog teeth spit. Apache tango. "I'll ride you Jack, I'll ride you 'til you die, I'll buck the song of God 'til you die between my legs." I taste my own blood charge, animal musk and sweat rush. The raw door of the mad dog is open and I'm riding the beast out of his gate. I'm riding him so hard I feel the drug spinning me in and out of delirium's rage. I come and I come and I come. Wet thirst and shell fire. Blasting scent from my open pores. I come blue wind on an opal sky. I ride your bones, Jack, 'til you can't move and I feel so hot, so hot, fairground of bruises over my body. She was a hothead, didn't see the traffic coming, so he got hit! Bam!

THE CHIMES STOP

I was twenty-two. I remember him running down my leg, he was running down my leg on the Greyhound headed home, warm and fresh. God, it was real good, forget or regret. So I forgot, but not him trying to break down the bathroom door with a pitchfork.

SHE TURNS
THE SKY ON HER SLIP HAS EXPANDED TO THE OTHER SLIPS
AND THE ENTIRE SCRIM
JANE WALKS INTO THE SKY

—BANFF, 1997

RED LIGHTNING

CONVERSATIONS WITH A CUNT

IN DREAM CLARA TALKS TO HER CUNT
HER BED TRANSFORMS IN A HUGE VULVA
SLOWLY THE VULVA STARTS ENGULFING HER
UNTIL EVENTUALLY IT SWALLOWS HER UP COMPLETELY

CLARA

Hello mon Popo

CLARA SPEAKS THE VOICE OF HER CUNT

CLARA (CUNT VOICE)

Hello
ma petite Sappho

CLARA

mon Popo
you're not dead

CLARA (CUNT VOICE)

Very much alive
ma petite Sappho
alive and kicking

Aren't you happy to see me

CLARA

Not particularly

CLARA (CUNT VOICE)

Set me a place at The Dinner Party
and let us eat

CLARA

I've been living a nun's love life so long
mon Popo
I thought you were dead

CLARA (CUNT VOICE)

Well, get that out of your head
you're at the height of your sex prime
for God's sake
ma petite Sappho
let's go
we got important work to do

Don't bury me before I am dead
I'm pleading play with me, baby
pick me up and take me to bed

Use my primordial lips
open your mouth wide and then scream
let me be your nuclear weapon free sex zone
I wanna be your wet dream
for God's sake
are you listenin' to me

I hope I don't sound desperate
but are you listenin'

CLARA

O mon Popo
my poor lonely archipelago

CLARA (CUNT VOICE)

Come swim
in the sweet cyprine

CLARA

I can't swim
you don't exist
this is only a dream

CLARA (CUNT VOICE)

Stop making sucky excuses
drag yourself up off the floor
and touch my a morphic juices

For Christ's sake
    I hope you're not going to make me beg

CLARA

Non
    mon Popo

CLARA (CUNT VOICE)

Yes
    ma petite Sappho

Get your mojo working
    stop moping around and lambada me
    for Christ's sake
    stop feeling sorry
    and hu-la-lu-ya me
        into infinity

Is that enough poetry for ya?
    am I turnin' you on?

Come on
    get mad and finger me
    or I'm gonna swallow you up
    and you'll only have one mouth
    how will that be
    only having one mouth to do all your talking
    and that'll be me

Think about it
    there's not a lot of alternatives
    I'm just goin' berserk

You're startin' to agro me here
    why should I do all the work

CLARA

Non
    mon Popo

CLARA (CUNT VOICE)

Yes
    ma petite Sappho

Stop trying to sweet-talk me sugar
    you're playing a sick game
    with the overseer of lip service

Either you come through
    or I'm going to swallow you
    bottom line
    get me off
    or I take you out

CLARA

Non
    mon Popo

CLARA (CUNT VOICE)

Yes
    ma petite Sappho

CLARA

No

CLARA (CUNT VOICE)

Yes
    I swallow
    you

CLARA

No

CLARA (CUNT VOICE)

Yes
I swallow you
    whole

CLARA

No . . .

CLARA'S CUNT SWALLOWS CLARA WHOLE
LAUGHING

—SEATTLE, 1998

THE ROOSTERS OF RAROTONGA

slow tide rests on the still day – aureole reef
round the naked neck of morning – like a flower lei
cloth slides off her shoulder
as she rolls between sheets – satin as shark skin
Cock-a-doodle-do
outside her window the rooster goes off – clock wise
Maori morning mantra – the call wakes the tree – she hears a thunk
reminds her of the sign – in the grove where tourists walk – reading palms
watch out for falling coconuts, she thinks
at that moment do you look up or down
she touches her breast with the tips of her fingers
Cock-a-doodle-do
further away another answers
cockeyed – he's older
his voice breaks – the sound of a hard night after a hard-knock life
she wakes from hip-shaking hula dreams
in a house between papaya and mango trees
waist-length black hair blows into the wind – window open – brushes her
strand by strand – she and the wind are intimate
have been for some time – curl and wind around each other's minds
embrace in hurricanes

another rooster picks up the call – and keeps going
cocking and cocking – poppycock cockiness – out of control
once he gets started he just can't stop
the feathers on his head turn red in the morning light
she's glad her bed is far enough away – he pleases her at a distance
her sand-softened foot touches down
as she slips into waking – the scent of frangipani
flowers float on air – edible rising

and further away the next rooster Cock-a-doodle-do's
on her side of the island he hardly exists – he's a lazy one
doesn't care if he rises – doesn't care if anyone rises
birds squabble over coconuts
by two corners she opens a thin blue cloth
two wings spread on either side of her naked curves
she glances down at her sex – wraps oceans around her

Cock-a-doodle-do
the Roosters of Rarotonga cock their way
'round the archipelago of her rising
slow – moving seduction into day
she ties a knot of blue between her breasts
coconuts are crazy, she thinks
they have a mind of their own
first roosters are close – their calls loud enough to feel
a cock tag team on the tiny island
she says, *can you see me underwater?*
O, I can smell you, coconut butter oil
she splashes her face with large open sweeps of water, sighs
they almost disappear and then one-by-one
they Cock-a-doodle-do
'til they settle down to roost
she thinks
no shoes today

—RAROTONGA, 1995

I'M SICK OF BEING A SEX TRAINER

"O yes, I've learned from my mistakes
I'm sure I could repeat them exactly"

—PETER COOK

I'm sick of being a sex trainer
teaching new dogs old dog tricks
if you gotta get whipped into shape
you got the wrong girl at the right gym
no more backwoods sex-lug hicks
no way
not in this girl's lucid love life
I swear, I'm not goin' there
if you don't have the goods
and throw them down right here
you can forget it
I'm movin' onto happier hormones

I'm sick of being a sex trainer
sick of teaching the bicycle
how to push and how to pull
sick of having to grade and fail
the unmiraculous with ego problems
who don't pay any attention to detail, no more
harder, more, softer, to the side
higher, lower, or go a little slower
no more *no, no, yes, no, no, no, yes, no, no, no, no, no*
I want a no-show knower
a G-spot go'er
a flame-eating thrower
in the shade
where the cool winds blow 'til we rise
bodies open, turn to steam

when I asked to be thrown on the bed
I did not ask for whip lash
I did not ask to be thrown across the room
to the wall on the other side of the bed

as a dry wall splat
I did not ask for that
I meant from *here*, not from *there*
here is here and there is there
it just isn't sexy, doesn't do it for me
going to the hospital, wearing a brace
because some spacecase decides to be romantic

I'm sick of being a sex trainer
psychoanalyst to a past love debate
if you got big problems, pay somebody, honey
I'm going first class air, no more travelling freight
good-bye whimpering and whining
so long snivelling and wailing
when undressed for fine dining
you gotta know what to order
you gotta know how you'd like it cooked
no more greedy grappling or needy sapling
look, I'd rather have a sandwich at home
alone

no more handing out scripts
to lovers who don't know what to say
here's your script, go memorize your lines
come say them back to me slow and low
and they do, and they forget their cues, halfway through, they corpse
can't remember the next line
and worse is when they get it in their heads
to improvise
good God, man
here I am, with my chair and my whip
and all you want is a little cat nip
and a fake toy mouse

I gotta tell you Dames out there
no more teaching trust to nervous animals
who get confused with two-word commands
the same thing over and over
no more rewarding the well-behaved with treats and hugs and pats

no more *give it, fetch, up* or *dinnertime*

One last tip, Dames, if you take this advice, you'll be alone
so remember this tip
they say
never go grocery shopping when you're hungry
I say
never work out when you're horny
you'll over do it
and injure yourself

—VICTORIA, 1998

FROM BUNHEAD TO BARD . . .

After a hard day of dancing
I'd pass the Bay Parkade everyday
I'd drag my worn-out bunhead butt home to lucky #3
My seventy-five-dollar-a-month room-tomb
With the shared yellowing bathroom

Sylis, the concert pianist turned junkie, dwelled down the hall

After a hard day of dancing
I'd pass Chinatown, and
I'd raid the dumpsters for tofu, and
I'd buy a bag of fortune cookies
For a broken moment of hookey from reality
Feeling like a disintegrating princess doll
Castle walls caving in
Tutu askew, and
A slew of unsatisfactory fortunes
In a bowl

After a hard day of dancing
I'd come home to lucky #3, and
I'd crack cookie after cookie
Looking for the perfect fortune, and
I'd dream about being a writer one day, and
Then I'd take my towel and walk down the hall
I'd have a bath and laugh at myself
'Cause I could never spell
How could I be a writer?

Unless
I have a table to write on
Yes
A room of one's own
Yes

So
The next day

I went to the Sally Ann
To look for a table to take away
Home to lucky #3
To write on
I found the perfect one
Round with flaps that swing down
I said to the Sally Ann Man:
This is my table
The perfect one for me
But there's no way to get it home to lucky #3
And the Sally Ann Man said:
Why don't I tie it on your back and you can carry it home
It's not far, and
Then you can write a poem or somethin'
(Seemed like a good idea at the time)
So he tied the rope around my leotards and tights
And off I trudged looking somewhat circus-like, with a twist

By the time I got to the Bay Parkade
I started feeling the table weight
Like Gregor in Kafka's Metamorphosis, and
My bladder was in a slightly urgent state
When I finally reached lucky #3
I thought I was going to pee
My leotards and tights
All over the floor in front of my door
I reached for my key, desperately

Then, incredulously
I realized I'd locked myself out, and
Then
My worst nightmare kicked in
Which took this scene on another downward spin
The Sally Ann Man had tied the knots on the other side of the flaps
On the other side of my wooden wings, and
There was no way I could reach them to untie the fuckin' things!
Now, I was tied to my own table
In a sense I was eternally trapped
Strapped to my own muse

Standing there in front of lucky #3
With the rising necessity to break down and pee

I walked down the hall to the shared bathroom there, and
I ripped down my leotards and tights through the roped-up snare,
And, then I gyrated toward the toilet bowl
Peeing all over myself, missing the hole
How could this happen to me
I started to cry
Then I heard myself yelling down the hallway
Why?
Why?
Why?

I manoeuvred the dance gear back up, and
Now with pee all over me
All I could think of was getting back to lucky #3
Squish
Squish
Squish

By now the table was just too much to hold
So I thought
I know, I'll . . .
yes, yes, o, yes
. . . just jump backwards onto the table-top for a rest
Yes, just jump backwards, that would be best
Wait for something to happen
Someone will help
yes

But once on top there was to way to get back on my feet, and
When my landlord finally found me
Locked out, tied up, smelling outhouse sweet
There was absolutely no way I could be . . . discreet

After he released me from the table's ugly hold
He said:
If I could be so bold
How would you like a date sometime?

I said:
Sorry I haven't time, you see
I've gotta set up my table
I've gotta write

Right
I've gotta right
Right
Alright
Right
Right
Have to write
Right . . .

—VANCOUVER, 1996

. . . AND BACK AGAIN

for Michele Moss

CALL/RESPONSE BETWEEN SPEAKER & DANCER/
DANCER & SPEAKER

Right
I gotta write
I gotta right to write
I gotta right to write
I gotta write
                                        right
I gotta write
                                        right

ENTER MUSIC

And the drum starts beating
                                        and the drum starts beating
and the drum starts beating
                                        and the drum starts beating
the drum is alive, beating out of its skin
                                        moves, woman-spine, starts slitherin'
supernatural speak, sweet serpent
and the XX sluices
                                        and the snake charmin' juices
electro-eroto-flow, eroto-flow, electro-
                                        unstrap those satin ribbons, let go
                                        let go, let go, let go

DOUBLE JEMBA HIT
HAND ON SKIN

tonk/tonk
makes you kick up the dark /tonk/tonk
makes you lick up the sparks /tonk/tonk
makes you dust off the dust
makes you hoodoo's bride

O snake woman slide, like honey
like honey, honey, like honey
like honey, honey, like honey
tonk/tonk
woman rattle and shake /tonk/tonk
women rattle and shake
in a crazy wisdom that slides –
that vibrates the hips, that seduces, that trips, that rides
grace revin', Harley, sweet daughter of heaven
In—hail—In—hail—In—hail
put your points on the fire, tune up your desire
X—hail—X—hail—X—hale

TEMPO SHIFT

and the music stays and the words start walkin' in time
making patterns from the page to the floor, dobra hips
start shakin' now, outta the poem, in a deathless wish to be cobra
so dobra mon cobra, fan blowing red ribbons at your nipples, lashing
ripples, rising outta the tropical moto with a breeze, hips shakin' like
the palms in the trees in a Rarotongian hurricane, ha ha ha ha to the
sand bard, between lips, fingers of fate snake, no mistake, like a cat,
civet, like a cat, civet

HANDS RESOUND IN AROUSED TIME

gong/gong/ga/gong/gong/gong
HIT IT!
Civet!

gong/gong/ga/gong/gong/gong
HIT IT!
Civet!

moving hands, hitting the make-
ker
hitting the make-
ker
hitting the make-
ker

on the ass
on her bare ass

on her bare ass

on her bare-

asanas open to the orphic woman speak
beat
heart leaves the cloud electrical in
moves delivered by the moon

by the moon

skin-cloth slow slides off the naked shoulder
of self breaking through, head dead/dead/dead first
dressed in new skin, opiately thin, in –
the language of twilight sky, flippin' inside outside in
ha

SHE FALLS TO HER KNESS
FOLLOW HER WITH OUTSPOKEN HANDS
SKIN PULSE BENDING BACK

when you drum the heat builds from the inside as a fever
a trance – from the inside burning out of you –

EXPOSES HER THROAT TO THE FURY
WET IN HUMID DANCE HEAT
WHITE SHIRT TIED ABOVE NAVEL
STICKS TO HER SOAKING BREASTS
TEMPLES TRACE SENDING HER INTO THE DRUM ITSELF
HER DANCE IS THE SOUND

leavin' blood on the drum

dance through it

leavin' blood on the drum

dance through it

the drum is alive beating out of its skin
and the blood is dreaming
and the drum is bleeding

is dreaming

is bleeding

dreaming

ha

doing everything but thinking now outta my mind wordless lines
between two poets all there is is wet 'til all there is is wet is wet
dye running down the apocryphal cloth of the body in a soma lick
of liquid jade a gynergy of body into words
of words on the body into praise

ball change

ha ha

step step

get down

get it down

get up to go down

get it down

dance

to

gether

three

for

nothing

(1 – 2 – 3 /2 – 2 – 3 /3 – 2 – 3 /ha)

time loosens in rising olfactory open quim

more music the music

of jazz

the music of jazz

ovums the air

uni-

fi-cates the air in voices with civetone tongue

rest
with no sleep sweet

taste of a single pulse

angels in bellies receive the souls of the dead

and then it turns
spot!
and then it turns
spot! on the spot
look one way
turn the other
spot
g-
spot
g- spot

g-

spot
turn
h-

i-

j-

k
dance

dance

from bunhead to bard and back, again
re-
turn
sweet daughter of heaven
burn, in a fleshy orgy of sound
and it all speeds up

and it all slows down, to the ground
and it just gets hotter
it just keeps on getting hotter
sweet heavenly daughter
newborn

                                                it just gets hotter

hotter

                                                sweet heavenly daughter

hotter

                                                it just keeps on getting hotter

—VANCOUVER, 1998

RAPID FLASH

MONTREAL MONTREAL AND ONLY MONTREAL

This Montreal story
takes places in Montreal Montreal and only Montreal
and does not include food or drink

In this Montreal, Quebec and only Montreal, Quebec story
without food or drink
Oui banners hang from ropes and windows and balconies
leftover from the vote

They said, in Montreal you should try to speak French
or people will be mean to you
so I tried to order in French and in several restaurants
waitresses begged me to speak English
pleese, speak Ing-lish, yor Frren-sh iz orbull
perfect

O yes, the Montreal Montreal and only Montreal story
the Montreal shopping in Montreal – shopping story
found a witchy necklace
designed and made in Montreal by a Montrealer
which is perfect for my Montreal story
the necklace needed matching earrings
the clerk, who is also a Montrealer from Montreal
says in English – she'd have some made
perfect
we talk about design
I buy the necklace and split satisfied that tomorrow
I'd buy the matching Montreal designed and made
earrings from Montreal – in Montreal – tomorrow
perfect

To get a Montreal apartment
you have to have Montreal references
Montreal Montreal and only Montreal, references

Back to the story
It's tomorrow

I stop in to pick up my matching Montreal earrings
it's a different clerk who only speaks French
most unhelpful and not good in Montreal
I try in my worse-than-broken attempt at French
I've – come – for – my – matching – Montreal – earrings
she just doesn't understand what the fuck I'm talking about
and I don't understand what the fuck she's talking about
Montreal Montreal and only Montreal

finally I say to her
I'm sorry I don't speak French, but I'm from another country

she says
waihr are hue frum?

I say
Canada

there's a pause and I'm thinking
okay perfect
it could swing one way or the other
in Montreal
she starts laughing
my forchin cookeez ar'hin Frren-sh
yours ar'hin Ing-lish
we both crack up
the same way, fortunately
Montreal Montreal and only in Montreal

— MONTREAL, 1996

OUI ET NON

for Christian Vezina

ON ONE PLANE BETWEEN TWO WINGS
AN IMAGINARY LINE ACROSS THE PLAYING SPACE
GREEK-FRIEZE JAZZ

SHE: Oui

SHE ENTERS STAGE LEFT/MAKES THREE GESTURES FROM HER HEART TO STAGE RIGHT/I WANT TO SHARE MY HEART

SHE: Non

SHE STAYS FACING STAGE RIGHT/FIST TO HER DROPPED HEAD IN DRAMATIC ACCEPTANCE/DENIAL/YOU WILL NEVER UNDERSTAND

HE: Oui

HE ENTERS STAGE RIGHT/FACING HER WITH ENTHUSIASTIC EYES/YES/SHE LIFTS HER HEAD WHEN SHE HEARS HIS VOICE/THEIR EYES MEET

HE: Non

HE JUMPS BACK INTO THE STAGE RIGHT WING

SHE: Oui

SHE CHASES HIM THREE STEPS/OUTSTRETCHED HAND/SHE STOPS

SHE: Non

SHE TURNS TO AUDIENCE, GESTURES/FORGET IT/WITH RIGHT HAND

HE: Oui

HE REENTERS FACING HER/SHE TURNS TO FACE HIM/HE WAFFLES THREE TIMES/FROM SIDE TO SIDE IN A DRAWN-OUT "OUI"

HE: Non

HE TURNS TO FACE THE AUDIENCE

SHE: We know

SHE TURNS TO AUDIENCE/THROWING HIM MENTALLY OFF

HE: We know?

HE APPROACHES/LISTENING

SHE: We know

TO HIM

SHE: We know

TO THE AUDIENCE

HE: We know we know?

HE FACES HER

SHE: We know we know

SHE TAKES FOUR STEPS TOWARDS HIM/GESTURING FIRST TO THEIR CHESTS AND THEN TO THEIR HEADS/WE UNDERSTAND ONE ANOTHER

HE: Nothing!

THEY ARE FACING ONE ANOTHER

SHE: Nothing?

SHE REACHES OUT TOWARDS HIM

HE: Nothing!

HE TURNS TOWARDS THE AUDIENCE

SHE: We know nothing?

SHE TURNS TOWARDS THE AUDIENCE

HE: Oui!

HE REMAINS BLANK-FACED/MATTER-OF-FACT/BEAT

HE: M-m-m-maybe

HE TURNS HIS HEAD SLIGHT TOWARDS HER/UNSURE

SHE: Oui, we

SHE TAKES TWO STEPS PER OUI AND WE

SHE: Together

SHE IS BESIDE HIM/SHE SLIDES HER HAND INTO HIS HAND

HE: Oh yes, hand-in-hand

HE ROLLS HIS EYES/CLICHÉ ROMANCE

SHE: C'est (hot)

THEY SWING THEIR HANDS BACK AND FORTH

HE: C'est not (h)ot

HE STOPS THEIR HANDS MID-AIR DOWN STAGE/LOOKS AT HER/LOOKS DOWN AT THEIR HANDS

SHE: Très (h)ot

SHE LOOKS AT HIM/LOOKS DOWN AT THEIR HANDS

HE: We ought not

HE TAKES ONE LARGE STEP TOWARDS STAGE RIGHT/HIS LEFT HAND UP TO STOP HER THOUGHTS

SHE: Too hot?

SHE PUTS HER HAND ON HER HIP

HE: Na-na-na-na-na-na-na-na-no!

HE MOVES TOWARDS HER AS IF TO DEFEND HIS EGO

SHE: Ya-ya-ya-ya-ya-ya-yes

SHE WRAPS HIS ARM THROUGH HIS

SHE: This-is-my-together

SHE INTRODUCES HIM TO THE AUDIENCE

HE: Ohhh I love togethers

HE LEANS AWAY FROM HER/THEIR ARMS STILL LINKED

SHE: It's night

SHE YANKS HIM BACK CLOSE BY HER SIDE

SHE: As one

SHE LOOKS ROMANTICALLY AT HIM

HE: In one couple?

WITH LINKED ARMS/HE SHUFFLES AWAY

SHE: As one

SHE SLIDES HER FEET TO MEET HIS

HE: In a couple?

HE SLIDES HIS FEET AWAY

SHE: As one

SHE SLIDES HIS FEET TOWARDS HIS

SHE: In a whole

SHE ACCIDENTALLY STEPS ON HIS TOES

HE: Not!

HE FACES AUDIENCES/CROSSES HIS ARMS IN DEFIANCE

SHE: Oh, come on.

TO HIM

SHE: We're just a couple of . . .

SHE CROSSES TO STAGE LEFT/NINE STEPS

HE: Togethers?

HE STOPS HER IN HER TRACKS

SHE: Yes, as we . . .

SHE TURNS AROUND/TO FACE HIM

HE: Are together?

HE TAKES TWO STEPS TOWARDS HER

SHE: Oui

SHE TAKES ONE STEP TOWARDS HIM

HE: A set?

HE TAKES ONE STEP TOWARDS HER

SHE: Oui . . . we

SHE TAKES ONE STEP TOWARDS HIM

HE: A compilation

HE TAKES ONE STEP TOWARDS HER

SHE: Oui, oui, oui, set for life

SHE TAKES ONE STEP TOWARDS HIM

HE: A pair?

HE TAKES ONE STEP TOWARDS HER/EXCITEMENT

SHE: Of togethers . . .

SHE TAKES ONE STEP TOWARDS HIM

HE: Of togethers?!

HE TAKES ONE STEP TOWARDS HER

SHE: Yes

SHE TAKES ONE STEP TOWARDS HIM

HE: Ensemble?

SHE: Yes!

EVERYTHING SPEEDS UP

HE: Yes

HE TAKES ONE STEP TOWARDS HER

SHE: Oui!

SHE TAKES ONE STEP TOWARDS HIM

HE: Oui?

HE TAKES ONE STEP TOWARDS HER

SHE: *Oui*

THEY ARE ALMOST TOUCHING

HE: Oui!

SHE: Oui! L'amour!

SHE LIFTS UP HER ARMS IN ECSTASY

HE: Oh no

HE ROLLS HIS EYES/WALKS AWAY/STAGE RIGHT

SHE: Oui!

SHE JUMPS ON HIS BACK/SOBBING INTO HIM

HE: Oui, mais oui

HE STOPS/CONTINUES TO SOB

HE: Mais oui

HE TURNS TOWARDS HER

HE: Oui, mais oui

HE HOLDS HER HANDS

SHE: Oui?

SHE LOOKS AT HIM

HE: Oui

HE IS RESIGNED/BEAT

SHE: Non

HER EYES WIDEN

SHE: We're . . .

SHE STEPS BACKWARDS

HE: Growing

HE TAKES A STEP TOWARDS HER

SHE: Apart
SHE TAKES A STEP BACKWARDS

HE: Growing
HE TAKES A STEP TOWARDS HER

SHE: Apart
SHE TAKES A STEP BACKWARDS

HE: Close yes growing
THEY TAKE FIVE STEPS/TOGETHER/THE LOOK OF BALLROOM

SHE: No growing
SHE STOPS HIM

HE: Yes growing
THEY REMAIN FACING ONE ANOTHER

SHE: No
SHE PUTS HER HANDS ON HIS SHOULDERS
SHE: No
SHE SPINS HIM AROUND
SHE: No
SHE PUSHES HIM AWAY

HE: Non, ne me quitte pas
DRAMATIC/FIVE STEPS AWAY

SHE: Go die!
SHE TURNS TO THE AUDIENCE

HE: Goodbye
REACHES FOR HER/TWO STEPS AWAY

SHE: Stay!
SHE TAKES TWO STEPS TOWARDS HIM

HE: Non

SHE: Don't go!

SHE PUTS HER HAND IN HIS

HE: Go away!

PUSHES HER HAND AWAY/WALKS STAGE LEFT

SHE: Stay!

SHE CHASES HIM/GRABS HIS HAND

HE: We know!

HE BACKS HER UP TO CENTRE

SHE: No, we non we oui!!!

THEY ARE HAVING AN ARGUMENT OF OUI AND NONS UNTIL THEY ARE YELLING/SHE GOES OVER THE TOP/HE STOPS/ RAISES HIS EYEBROWS/SLOWLY TURNS TO STAGE LEFT/SHE TURNS TO STAGE RIGHT

HE: Red

THEY BOTH TAKE ONE STEP AWAY

HE: Et blanche

THEY BOTH TAKE ONE STEP AWAY

SHE: White

THEY BOTH TAKE ONE STEP AWAY

SHE: Et rouge

THEY BOTH TAKE ONE STEP AWAY

HE: And blue

THEY BOTH TAKE ONE STEP AWAY

she: Et bleu

THEY BOTH TAKE ONE STEP AWAY

HE: I got the blues
HE TAKES ONE STEP/HURT BODY WAVE

SHE: I got the bleu-
SHE TAKES ONE STEP/HURT BODY WAVE
SHE: Oui
SHE REACHES OUT TO HIM

HE: Non
HE STOPS HER/SHE TURNS AWAY

HE: Oui
SHE TURNS TO HIM

SHE: No

TOGETHER: Oui
THEY BOTH TAKE A STEP BACKWARDS
TOGETHER: No
THEY BOTH TAKE A STEP BACKWARDS
TOGETHER: Oui
THEY BOTH TAKE A STEP BACKWARDS
TOGETHER: No
THEY BOTH TAKE A STEP BACKWARDS

TOGETHER: Yes
THEY FACE EACH OTHER/SMILE
TOGETHER: We know
TOGETHER: Nothing
TO AUDIENCE

—QUEBEC CITY, 1997

SHERI-D WILSON is an international artist known for her innovative and dramatic performance style. She has performed her work in North America and Europe, and has held numerous workshops and lectures. Her play *Confessions: A Jazz Play* was performed at Tamahnous Theatre (Vancouver) and she co-created and performed *Boy Wonder* with Ballet B.C. She is the author of three previous books of poetry: *Bulls Whip and Lambs Wool* (Peterade Press), *Swerve* (Arsenal Pulp Press), and *Girl's Guide to Giving Head* (Arsenal Pulp Press). Sheri-D divides her time between Calgary and Vancouver.

ALSO AVAILABLE FROM
ARSENAL PULP PRESS

POETRY:

ARCHIVE FOR OUR TIMES *Dorothy Livesay; Dean J. Irvine, ed.*
Previously uncollected and unpublished poems by the late Dorothy Livesay, a legend of Canadian poetry, spanning her career from the 1920s to the 1980s. "An invaluable addition to the poet's ouevre. . . . These poems serve to remind the reader of Livesay's skill and vision." —*Quill & Quire*
1-55152-059-1; $19.95

KINGSWAY *Michael Turner*
A collection of linked poems about Vancouver's oldest thoroughfare. "Turner's work, like Kingsway, is an epic traversal, cris-crossed with beauty and trash." —LYNN CROSBIE
1-55152-028-1; $10.95

GIRL'S GUIDE TO GIVING HEAD *Sheri-D Wilson*
A dazzling and thoroughly modern collection that collapses convention in its search for the feminine. "Tragic and funny; Wilson is a gutsy modern broad." —*Vancouver Sun*
1-55152-031-1; $14.95 Cda / $12.95 U.S.

SWERVE *Sheri-D Wilson*
"This work understands the importance of giving honor to the anima, the feminine spirit, in fact the goddess." —MARIANNE FAITHFULL
0-88978-274-1; $12.95

RAGAS FROM THE PERIPHERY *Phinder Dulai*
"A genuine meeting of two cultures in poetry, beautifully and thoughtfully expressed." —*eyeWeekly*
1-55152-021-4; $12.95

FICTION:

ONCE UPON AN ELEPHANT *Ashok Mathur*

Brash and wickedly funny, this detective novel is a fantastical contemporary retelling of the creation story of Ganesh. "This novel will charm and enlighten all gods and humans interested in the world we really live in." —LARISSA LAI

1-55152-058-3; $16.95 Cda / $13.95 U.S.

CONTRA/DICTION *Brett Josef Grubisic, ed.*

An anthology of queer men's fiction, full of beauty and danger, that challenges the gay mainstream. "These stories convey an edginess and sense of risk often missing in Hollywoodized, homogenized images of gay men." —*Publishers Weekly*

1-55152-056-7; $18.95 Cda / $15.95 U.S.

AMERICAN WHISKEY BAR *Michael Turner*

The controversial and groundbreaking novel by the author of *Hard Core Logo*. "Brilliant: a dazzling, dizzying multilayered blend of fact and fiction." —*The Globe & Mail*

1-55152-048-6; $15.95

THE GHOST OF UNDERSTANDING *Jean Smith*

An intensely personal novel by the lead singer of Mecca Normal and one of the founders of the riot-grrrl movement. "Jean Smith is like a terrorist who demands you read all her diaries." —*Quill & Quire*

1-55152-050-8; $14.95 Cda / $12.95 U.S.

AND A BODY TO REMEMBER WITH *Carmen Rodríguez*

A luminous short-story collection based on the author's life as a Chilean exile in Canada. Winner of a City of Santiago Book Prize; shortlisted for the City of Vancouver Book Prize. "This collection underlines the power of the simple story." —*Vancouver Sun*

1-55152-044-3; $15.95 Cda / $12.95 U.S.

NON-FICTION:

ICE AND FIRE *Stephen Osborne*

A smart, funny, and moving collection of essays by the editor of the award-winning Canadian magazine Geist. "Stephen Osborne's spirited, stylish way of bringing reality into focus produces exceptionally readable and memorable prose." —ROBERT FULFORD

1-55152-061-3; $15.95

BAD JOBS *Carellin Brooks, ed.*

A raucous collection of stories and comics that depict, in gory true-life detail, bad jobs—from beet canning factory worker to Chinese food delivery boy, and everything in between.

1-55152-055-9; $16.95 Cda / $14.95 U.S.

NATIONAL DREAMS *Daniel Francis*

The stories behind the icons of Canadian history, from the RCMP to the CPR. "A brilliant examination of our national myths." —*Toronto Star*

1-55152-045-3; $19.95

VANCOUVER: SECRETS OF THE CITY *Shawn Blore*

A cheeky guidebook to Vancouver's best-kept secrets, from shopping and sightseeing to dining and clubbing, produced in conjunction with *Vancouver* magazine.

1-55152-062-1; $15.95

Ask for these and other great Arsenal Pulp Press titles at better bookstores. Or get them directly from the press (please add shipping charges: $3.00 for first book, $1.50 per book thereafter; Canadian residents add 7% GST):

ARSENAL PULP PRESS
103-1014 Homer Street
Vancouver, B.C.
Canada V6B 2W9

Also check out our website:
www.arsenalpulp.com